THE OLD TESTAMENT
IN THE CHURCH

THE OLD TESTAMENT
IN THE CHURCH

by

ALEXANDER NAIRNE, D.D.

✠

CAMBRIDGE
AT THE UNIVERSITY PRESS
1932

CAMBRIDGE
UNIVERSITY PRESS

University Printing House, Cambridge CB2 8BS, United Kingdom

Published in the United States of America by Cambridge University Press, New York

Cambridge University Press is part of the University of Cambridge.

It furthers the University's mission by disseminating knowledge in the pursuit of education, learning and research at the highest international levels of excellence.

www.cambridge.org
Information on this title: www.cambridge.org/9781107695993

© Cambridge University Press 1932

First published 1932
Re-issued 2014

A catalogue record for this publication is available from the British Library

ISBN 978-1-107-69599-3 Paperback

THE OLD TESTAMENT
IN THE CHURCH

That strange writer George Moore prefixed this dedication to that strange book *The Brook Kerith*:

My dear Mary Hunter,

It appears that you wished to give me a book for Christmas, but were in doubt what book to give me as I seemed to have little taste for reading, so in your embarrassment you gave me a Bible. It lies on my table now with the date 1898 on the fly-leaf—my constant companion and chief literary interest for the last 18 years. Itself a literature, it has led me into many various literatures and into the society of scholars. I owe so much to your Bible that I cannot let pass the publication of *The Brook Kerith* without thanking you for it again. Yours always: George Moore.

Is not that a fine appreciation and example? The Bible is itself a literature, and another veteran of letters (George Saintsbury) has testified of literature thus:

...Some may say, "Oh! this is frivolous, at best it is literature, not religion". Well, Sir, for my part I hold that of all exercises of human faculty Literature and Art "tread nearest to God", and I think the more we can avail ourselves of their company in His service the better.

And the Bible introduces to other literatures, opens the gate of the Republic of letters. No one who studies the Bible fails to attempt further studies. If, scarce studying, we are frequent readers of the Bible we become scholarly in thought and language, our mind is deepened, simplified, ennobled, we "tread nearest to God" and that forms character. And the Bible carries us into larger spaces than mere letters, for the Bible is the one book which is still read aloud, publicly, in Church, and so passes into open air and the active life of men. So it comes that a God-fearing country labourer speaks the most authentic English of us all, and is unconsciously steeped in poetic sacramental reverie—as country parsons know who read the Bible much and parasitical literature little, meditating and studying a few rather than reading many books. The Bible is the grandest literature because it is The Vulgar Tongue.

George Moore makes us notice another point. *The Brook Kerith* is a Life of our Lord Jesus Christ, and a fine Life; yes and reverent, though unorthodox and very bold. But the point is that the whole Bible led him to the Gospel as the centre, and from the Gospel he contemplates the whole. That surely is right. A child should make his first start, and we all should renew our thought and study every day, with the Gospel. Our thought about God and forgiveness and eternal life and our human duties and affections must spring from the pure fount, not from the distant subterranean waters. First the life and teaching of our Lord, then the Old Testament as introductory and the rest of the New Testament as interpretation and application.

But, if secondary, these are not the less necessary. In Dr A. E. Abbott's *Silanus the Christian* we read of a young Roman nobleman attending the lectures of Epictetus. Dissatisfied, he comes across certain of S. Paul's epistles. Partly understanding, he enquires of his bookseller—Who is this Paul? Who is the Christ Jesus of whom he writes? The bookseller can tell him of the Gospels and gets him one. Still the Gospel requires introductory explanation, and he becomes acquainted with Isaiah and some other pieces of the Old Testament, the Bible of the Jewish Church and of our Lord.

Something like that should be our way with those "children of the Church" for whom Canon Dalton gives us that tender Collect in his noble edition of The Book of Common Prayer.

So, we need not forbid our nursery students of the Gospel the exquisite stories of Genesis even from their earliest days. The Child Jesus read these stories, and if English children would learn his mind they should read them too. Only I would plead for the very words of Genesis, not a paraphrase; and the story, not much explanation: children catch the poetry better than their teachers can.

The Old Testament was our Lord's Bible, but he seems to have used generally a part of it only: he had his own Shorter Bible. Genesis Exodus Deuteronomy Psalms and Prophets sufficed him. Such selection is critical, and the Sermon on the Mount shews what a bold critic he was. But notice that his criticism is constructive, creative. He does not destroy, he is not didactic, does not lecture: he restores, renews, puts life into conventions, persuades by fresh reality, rouses that warm curiosity for truth which is the impulse of scholarship. We clergy ought to know the gist of the last 50 years' critical work on Old Testament, we ought to take some pains to get a clear general view. But we ought not to make the worshipping faithful share our pains when we preach to them: sermons must not be lectures: there are other places and times for lectures.

Nor should we be offensive and waste time in correcting what we think errors about dates and authorship—that is not the way of literature in which we tread close to God. Once more, set the Gospel in the centre; preach the Saviour and salvation; turn the Old Testament always that way; and do this all the clearer and more winningly because you know the history, the progressive revelation of the Old Testament, more accurately than our grandfathers did. That will forbid our saying some things: it will make us put some things in a way that before our critical studies we should not have put them. But there is no need to spend 10 of our precious 20 minutes in explaining why we do so; and if we skip that unnecessary explanation few will notice that we have turned critics—no one will be shocked: on the other hand, if we have taken pains with our proper message—our Evangel—it will go forth with tenfold power and charm:—The law was given by Moses, grace and truth came through Jesus Christ.

The victory of criticism is already won by those who read the Hebrew Bible or arrange their English version with its titles and in its order. Those elaborate titles of authorship—first book of Moses, etc.—disappear: each book is designated simply by its opening words—"In the beginning" and so on: "The Lamentations of Jeremiah" is just "Ah!" More significant is the position of that poem, far away from the prophecies and history of Jeremiah in the third division or volume of the Bible of the Synagogue. For that Bible is in three volumes: I *Tora* or Law, i.e. Genesis to Deuteronomy; II *Nebi'im* or Prophets, i.e. Joshua Judges Samuel Kings (not Chronicles) and, with these prophetic histories, Isaiah Jeremiah Ezekiel and the "Book of the xii"—Hosea to Malachi, but not Daniel. Daniel, which is written partly in the later Palestinian dialect, Aramaic, and is plainly connected in some way with the rising of the Maccabees against Antiochus Epiphanes in the 2nd century B.C., comes in the last volume,

Kethubim or Writings, where Job Psalms Ecclesiastes and the rest of our books are placed. This last volume seems to have been still vaguely defined in the apostolic age, and in that age the conservative Sadducees accepted only the Law as canonical, disapproving of the Pharisees and their reverence for The Prophets—the people's book.

But this grows tedious. Any one—if there be any—to whom it is new can work out the hint for themselves. The hint is that the three volumes represent three dates in the forming of the Canon, and roughly point to the dates of their contents. When Ezra read the Law in the restored Jerusalem the Jewish *Bible* was inaugurated: but before that an earlier *Prophetic Book of the Covenant* which was found in the Temple (according to the history in Kings) had been composed and became all but authoritative. Thus we may read the *Nebi'im* as more or less contemporary documents of the story and the theology therein contained; the *Tora* as the Law of Moses in its full exilic developement; and the *Kethubim* as a postexilic collection of late books (though early pieces may be included in the late collections, especially in the Psalter).

That is the dry line for following out the hint. But most people who care in student fashion for Old Testament have got beyond that to-day. They are already freed from undue anxiety about the letter, and desire practical application to history or theology: to read the history of Israel truly, or to learn truly how it affects the promise of the Gospel—as Uncle Toby says in *Tristram Shandy*, "What has this to do with a man who fears GOD?"

Instruction is one of the duties of the Church to the people. Sermons are only one of the means for fulfilling that duty. I would gladly see some of the energy with which we defend Church day schools diverted to the establishment of biblical and theological Continuation Classes. I wish our old and hitherto excellent Bible Classes raised to the efficiency to-day demanded in secular subjects like Natural Science. That needs a reading

thinking clergy: *Clerus Anglicanus stupor mundi*—
why not make that praise good again? We might
do so as scholars ourselves or as patrons of scholarship, for laymen would readily realise their
"priesthood of the laity"—"a royal priesthood
an holy nation"—by teaching things they really
know, and we should be exercising our pres-
byteral priesthood in selection and welcome. But
selection would involve many rejections, and on
the whole the privilege is ours, and the people
would like us to make much of it; English people
respect a studious parish priest.

Let me sketch a plan of study for such a class in
Old Testament.

There will be three years' work, three leisurely
full years of conversation as well as instruction:

      I The period of the Prophets.
     II The Exile and the making of the Bible.
    III Second thoughts on Genesis—Deu-
        teronomy.

I After a glance at Joshua and Judges, so as to

set Israel in Canaan, read Samuel and Kings through. Here and there dull tracts will interrupt the vivid history and the conductor will learn and practise the scholarly art of skipping. On the other hand he will, for himself, read mark learn and inwardly digest all the books of the prophets, and especially Amos Hosea Isaiah Jeremiah Ezekiel; so that he can readily quote, from memory, the words of the prophets as vivid illustrations of the story. This division possesses vividness throughout, but the prophets' words are more vivid than the historian's art can ever be— the very words of very actors on the scene, actual voices from the drama. The story begins with Israel enslaved to Philistine, like Italy to Austria. Monarchy and Prophecy spring out of the nation's need; it is Israel's *Risorgimento*. Then the characters of Saul and David, the empire of Solomon, the revolt of puritan Israel against the clan of Judah. Then corruption of faith and manners, oppression of poor, degeneration of national character: judgement for purging: the tyranny of

Assyria: Amos Hosea Isaiah: the end of Northern Israel, that romantic race of Highland-men.

Then Judah and the Temple left, and the house of David, with its Stuart-like fatality. The empire of Babylon: Judah's revolt and ruin: Jeremiah Habakkuk Ezekiel.

This sketch may give a faint idea of the interest which such a lesson in history might rouse. But read one modern book for stimulus and aid—Robertson Smith's *Prophets of Israel*. Some boy perhaps will join the class at that age when boys are least religious. He will be surprised to find such rousing history in the Bible. It is likely that he will end this first year by seeing in the history and politics the present action of the Living GOD; as the prophets did; as Robertson Smith shews them doing.

II Jerusalem fell. The Chaldeans carried the better part of the Judeans into captivity. Jeremiah stayed to share the low estate of the remnant. Ezekiel watched the tragedy from Babylon where he was already shepherding a company of earlier exiles. Now, at once, in the utter darkness, he changes prophecy to hope, and prepares for restoration and regeneration by fashioning a brief Leviticus, codifying ancient Law, modifying it for new times, and revealing deeper ideas of sacrifice as atonement, cleansing, renewal of the heart with GOD. He is the first Scribe. He inaugurates the Bible of the Jewish Church.

The *Tora* and *Kethubim* shew us what the thought and doubt and piety of the exilic Church was: *Tora* with its history of Israel's divine origin and destiny; Job and Ecclesiastes with their meditative questioning; Psalter, the Prayer Book of house and synagogue, quiet patient exultant trustful—literature treading nearest to God, pregnant with the Christ—not just "The LORD's Anointed" as Saul and David had been, but "The Christ who is to be".

The second part of the Book of Isaiah, the "Comfort Ye" prophecy shews how 50 years of such an exile had deepened Israel's theology.

Jahveh is here the one Lord, the Creator and Saviour of the Nicene Creed. The Old Testament faithfully records the fierce cruelties of early Israel, the pagan superstitions of popular religion —*Sheol* and the like—but itself, the Bible of the Jewish Church, does not endorse that superstition and stiffneckedness. It enshrines the maturing faith of the "Jews" (as this people have since styled themselves in a fine pride of humility). Therefore—

The Old Testament is not contrary to the New: for both in the Old and New Testament everlasting life is offered to Mankind by Christ, who is the only Mediator between God and Man, being both God and Man. Wherefore they are not to be heard, which feign that the old Fathers did look only for transitory promises.[1]

If you still read that article of our religion with misgiving, read Cheyne, that drastic and most religious critic: read his *Bampton Lectures on the Psalter*, his *Commentary on the Psalms* (the first

[1] Article VII.

edition, in one volume), his *Job and Solomon*, his *Jewish Religious Life after the Exile*.

III Then, after all this discipline, we come back to Genesis and Exodus. Come back: for of course we listened to the Hymn of Creation and Abraham and Jacob and Esau, and Egypt and the Bulrushes and the Red Sea, yes, and the Tower of Babel, when we were little children, and we delighted in it all. But then, whether our elders explained too much, or original sin must have its way, we ate of the tree of knowledge, distinguished between history and romance, judged these fables to be no longer "true", and lost taste for them and put them away with other childish things. So may *Paradise Lost* seem to a young man musical, but too naïve a paraphrase of worn-out legend to engage the deepening speculation of his mind. And so, even as he returns to *Paradise Lost* after reading Milton's *de Doctrina Christiana*, and recognises Milton's bold philosophy strongly interposed with the sonorous poetry, and the whole demanding the utmost effort and attention of his intellect—so do we, after we have studied Israel's eventful story, and learned how kings interact with prophets, and a profoundly progressive revelation of the living God has thus emerged, and how the *Tora*—Genesis—Leviticus—Deuteronomy—is not the childish primal lisping, but very flower and completion of the long process—so we come back and read the stories, and the rubrics of Leviticus, and the sermon of Deuteronomy, with freshened understanding. The six-days' creation is no longer a discredited piece of history or natural science, but the magnificent Hymn of Creation, the poetic creed of the Jewish Church, with its adoration of the one transcendent Spirit, God, and its awestruck humble daring faith that man is akin to God, *Imago Dei*. When presently those genial Rabbis, the composers of the Bible, refuse to rob the children of the Tower of Babel and the nine preliminary plagues of Pharaoh, we are to remember that the Hymn of Creation is the Church's confession of the one very God, and

interpret these arabesques by that holy serious-
ness. When we read of Jacob wrestling at the
Brook Jabbok, we may enjoy the vigour of the
story telling; we may or may not track the story
back to some rude piece of folklore, but we shall
remember what penetrating reverie hallowed the
Bible-making Church of the Exile, and freely
recognise the theology of the narrative in Genesis
—There stands the Christ—in a mystery—as yet
(like Him who spoke to Moses from the Bush) he
will not tell his name: " Wherefore is it that thou
dost ask after my name ?"—"I am—that I am".

Yet this intellectual reading—reverent—intellectual though it be—is not perfect appreciation. The returner to *Paradise Lost* wrongs Milton
if his return is predominantly theological. The
poem is predominantly an Epic, a story. Under,
or rather fused with that, is the drama of Christ
and Satan, Reason and Passion, battling for the
soul of every man. But the battle is a battle, and
both the champions are to be admired with awe,
pity, infinite wonder, breathless expectancy—

In dubioque fuere utrorum ad regna cadendum
omnibus humanis esset terraque marique[1]

While the fate of all mankind still hangs uncertain to
which Lord it must fall; the eternal issue shrouded
by space and time:

and the genuinely Miltonic reader is rapt by the
story.

So with the story of the patriarchs. It means
eternal things, but it is a story still: will you not
say The Story, the only great universal story of
the primeval world? Is the *Iliad* its equal? The
classical scholar answers "Yes, and far more than
equal", but he answers in his haste. "All great
art is praise" is a masterful aphorism, and the narrative of Genesis is praise in a closer sense than
the phrase can be used of any pagan art. We cannot say that of the whole Old Testament against
the whole of Hellenic literature, but take each at
its highest instance, and at least we dare to put
the question.

Somehow we have wandered back to where

[1] Lucretius, III, 836.

we started, to the Old Testament as literature. And perhaps that admonishes us no more to indulge in vain antitheses. For our part let us hold that "of all exercises of human faculty Literature and Art tread nearest to God". This is especially to be received and valued in Old Testament. There is another critical aphorism, or household word, of readers: "Great eloquence convinces not by persuasion but by rapture".[1] You catch the meaning of that if you think of the Revelation of S. John the Divine or of certain outbursts of S. Paul. But the Old Testament abounds in such sublimities; grandeur is its prerogative. No doubt there is a finer way of speaking still. Who would talk of eloquence or persuasion or rapture when he listens to the Lord Jesus? No one would compare Job with that. No, nor yet with Jacob at the well. Next to the Gospels Genesis is the most beautiful literature in the world.

And it is worth while to win back the mind and ear and tongue of the young generation to this

[1] Longinus, *On the Sublime*, I, 4.

beauty. Nor should the task be difficult; for this is their native art. English people have always had open ears for the spoken word. Never have they achieved supremacy in music painting sculpture building. But the stream of poetry runs ever freshly through England's life. And there is no version—at least since Jerome's fragrant Latin Vulgate—that comes near the English Bible; in the Revised more close to truth than in the Authorised, and still excellent in phrase and rythm. Read the opening paragraphs of Chapter VIII in J. R. Green's *Short History of the English People*, and see how their Bible affected Englishmen at the Revival of Learning. Here was for them the heart of the Renascence. And a new Renascence is burgeoning in Europe to-day.

This paper is meant to be practical. It is addressed to active servants of the Church: *ad clerum* but not *infra claustrum*. Therefore I have not named many books. If more detailed accuracy in historical statement or more penetrative analysis of doctrinal developement be desired, I would refer to the chapters in *The Cambridge Ancient History*, vols. I, II, III and VI on the Semites; Syria and Palestine; Israel, Judah, the Prophets; the Inauguration of Judaism; by that finely philosophic scholar Dr Stanley Cook. The notes with which he has enriched his new edition of Robertson Smith's *Religion of the Semites* provide latest knowledge and original reflexion on many subjects of serious interest.

Dr Kennett's *Old Testament Essays* also deal with some of the most insistent problems of history and religion in the Old Testament, and may correct a few lines in this paper where I have been content to repeat a generally accepted sequence in chronology. Dr Kennett would perhaps judge my vagueness more severely, and his own erudite honesty demands attention. And he is as good to read as Dr Cook, in his very idiosyncratic style, rousing enthusiasms like his own in his disciples.

www.ingramcontent.com/pod-product-compliance
Ingram Content Group UK Ltd.
Pitfield, Milton Keynes, MK11 3LW, UK
UKHW031824020325